Songwriting

A Beginner's Guide to Writing Great Lyrics in Under a Day

Written By: Julian Patterson

Table of Contents

Introduction

Welcome to "Songwriting Made Easy: A Beginner's Guide to Writing Great Lyrics in Under a Day". This book is designed for aspiring songwriters who want to learn how to write powerful, meaningful lyrics that resonate with their audience. Whether you're a seasoned musician looking to sharpen your skills or a beginner who's just starting out, this book will provide you with the tools and techniques you need to write great songs in a short amount of time.

In this book, we'll cover everything from the basics of songwriting to more advanced topics like melody, arrangement, and recording. We'll also explore different musical genres and show you how to adapt your writing style to fit each one. Additionally, we'll discuss copyright and legal issues related to songwriting, as well as marketing strategies for getting your music heard by the right people.

By the end of this book, you'll have a solid understanding of what it takes to write great lyrics and create powerful, memorable songs that connect with your audience. So, whether you're writing for your own enjoyment or hoping to break into the music industry, let's get started on your songwriting journey!

Chapter 1: Understanding the Basics

Introduction

Songwriting is a craft that involves many different elements, from melody and harmony to lyrics and form. Understanding the basics of songwriting is crucial for anyone looking to write compelling, memorable songs that connect with audiences. In this context, the three subtopics that are essential for understanding the basics of songwriting include elements of songwriting, developing songwriting skills, and song structure and form. The elements of songwriting are the building blocks that help create the structure and meaning of a song. Developing songwriting skills involves honing one's abilities to craft melody, lyrics, and other components of a song. Finally, understanding song structure and form is key to creating coherent, effective songs that engage listeners. In the following sections, we will delve into each of these subtopics in more detail.

Elements of Songwriting

Elements of songwriting refer to the various building blocks or components that make up a song. These elements include melody, harmony, rhythm, and lyrics. Understanding these elements is crucial for songwriters who want to create a compelling and memorable song that resonates with their audience.

The melody is the most prominent and recognizable aspect of a song. It refers to the series of notes that form the tune or the "hook" of the song. A strong melody is often catchy, memorable, and emotionally resonant, and can help make a song stand out in a crowded field of competing music.

Harmony refers to the way multiple notes and melodies interact with each other to create a fuller, more complex sound. Harmonies can add depth, texture, and emotion to a song, and can help create a sense of movement or progression as the song develops.

Rhythm is the element of songwriting that creates a sense of time, flow, and motion within the song. A strong rhythm can make a song feel more energetic and engaging, while a more subdued rhythm can create a sense of calm and introspection.

Lyrics are the words that accompany the melody, and are often the most direct way that songwriters can communicate their message and connect with their audience. Good lyrics should be compelling, memorable, and emotionally resonant, and should work in harmony with the melody to create a cohesive and impactful song.

Understanding the elements of songwriting is not only important for creating a great song, but also for communicating effectively with collaborators or other musicians. By having a solid grasp of these elements, songwriters can better express their ideas and work more effectively with others to create the best possible songs.

In summary, mastering the elements of songwriting is essential for aspiring songwriters who want to create memorable, emotionally resonant music that connects with their audience. By paying attention to the melody, harmony, rhythm, and lyrics, songwriters can create songs that stand out and leave a lasting impression on their listeners.

Developing Songwriting Skills

Developing songwriting skills involves honing one's abilities to craft melody, lyrics, and other components of a song. Songwriters can improve their skills by practicing their craft regularly, experimenting with different techniques and styles, and seeking feedback and collaboration from other musicians.

One of the most important aspects of developing songwriting skills is cultivating a strong sense of creativity and inspiration. This can involve seeking out new experiences, exploring different genres of music, and being open to new ideas and perspectives. Many successful songwriters also engage in improvisation and freestyle writing as a way to generate fresh ideas and break through writer's block.

Another key aspect of developing songwriting skills is learning the technical aspects of music theory, including chord progressions, scales, and song structures. By understanding these fundamentals, songwriters can craft songs that are harmonically interesting, musically coherent, and emotionally resonant.

Collaboration can also be a powerful tool for developing songwriting skills. By working with other musicians and writers, songwriters can learn new techniques, gain different perspectives, and refine their ideas. Collaborators can provide feedback on lyrics, melody, and other components of the song, helping to refine and improve the final product.

Finally, it is important for songwriters to be persistent and dedicated to their craft. Developing songwriting skills takes time and effort, and success is often the result of hard work and perseverance. By staying committed to their goals and continuing to hone their craft, songwriters can create music that resonates with their audience and leaves a lasting impact.

In conclusion, developing songwriting skills is a vital aspect of becoming a successful songwriter. Through regular practice, experimentation, collaboration, and dedication, songwriters can hone their abilities to craft compelling, emotionally resonant songs that connect with their audience.

Song Structure and Form

Song structure and form refer to the organization and arrangement of different components within a song. This includes the verse, chorus, bridge, intro, and outro, among others. Understanding song structure and form is important for songwriters, as it can help create a cohesive and engaging song that keeps the listener's attention.

One common structure for a song is the verse-chorus form, in which the song alternates between a verse section, which typically tells a story or conveys a message, and a chorus section, which features a memorable melody and lyrics that are repeated throughout the song. This structure is often used in pop, rock, and folk music, and is known for its accessibility and catchiness.

Another popular song structure is the AABA form, which features an initial verse (A), followed by a repeated verse (A), then a contrasting section (B), and finally a return to the initial verse (A). This structure is often used in jazz and show tunes, and is known for its sense of progression and resolution.

Bridge sections are another important aspect of song structure, providing a contrast to the verse and chorus sections and often featuring a different chord progression and melody. Bridges can add emotional depth to a song and help create a sense of movement or tension.

In addition to these common structures, songwriters can also experiment with unconventional forms, such as changing time signatures, adding unexpected sections, or rearranging the traditional structure of a song.

Overall, understanding song structure and form is important for creating a cohesive and engaging song that resonates with the listener. By paying attention to the different sections of a song and how they work together, songwriters can create music that tells a compelling story, evokes emotion, and captures the listener's attention from beginning to end.

Conclusion

In conclusion, understanding the basics of songwriting is essential for anyone looking to become a successful songwriter. Through exploring the three subtopics of elements of songwriting, developing songwriting skills, and song structure and form, we can begin to understand the foundational components of songwriting. By mastering the elements of songwriting, such as melody, harmony, and lyrics, songwriters can create songs that are both musically and lyrically compelling. Developing songwriting skills, such as improvisation and experimentation, allows for growth and expansion of the craft. Understanding song structure and form provides a roadmap for creating a cohesive and engaging song that captures the listener's attention. Together, these subtopics form the backbone of songwriting and can help aspiring songwriters to unlock their potential and create music that resonates with audiences.

Chapter 2: Finding Inspiration

Introduction

Songwriting is a deeply personal and creative endeavor that requires inspiration and creativity. Finding inspiration is often the first step towards creating a great song, and it can come from a variety of sources. Exploring different art forms can be a valuable way to find inspiration, as it exposes songwriters to different styles and techniques that they can incorporate into their own work. Embracing life experiences is another important source of inspiration, as personal stories and emotions can be powerful tools for creating music that resonates with listeners. Finally, seeking collaboration and feedback can help songwriters to expand their creative horizons and refine their ideas, providing valuable insight and perspective from other musicians and industry professionals.

Exploring Different Art Forms

Exploring different art forms is an essential way for songwriters to find inspiration and create music that is unique and fresh. There are many different art forms that can provide inspiration for songwriters, including visual arts, literature, film, and other musical genres.

Visual arts, such as painting, sculpture, and photography, can be a rich source of inspiration for songwriters. The colors, shapes, and textures found in visual art can inspire new musical ideas, while the themes and emotions conveyed in the artwork can provide a starting point for songwriting.

Literature, including poetry, fiction, and non-fiction, can also be a valuable source of inspiration for songwriters. The imagery, themes, and language found in literature can inspire new lyrics and melodies, while the emotions and stories conveyed in the written word can provide a basis for songwriting.

Film and television can also provide inspiration for songwriters. The visuals, themes, and emotions conveyed in movies and TV shows can spark new musical ideas, while the stories and characters can provide a basis for songwriting.

Exploring different musical genres is another important way to find inspiration for songwriting. Listening to music from different cultures, time periods, and genres can expose songwriters to new rhythms, melodies, and chord progressions that they can incorporate into their own work. Collaborating with musicians from different genres can also be a valuable way to find new inspiration and create music that is fresh and unique.

Overall, exploring different art forms can help songwriters find new inspiration, and create music that is unique, engaging, and emotionally resonant. By paying attention to the different art forms around them, songwriters can discover new ideas and perspectives that can inform their work, and help them create music that truly stands out.

Embracing Life Experiences

Embracing life experiences is an essential way for songwriters to find inspiration and create music that is deeply personal and emotionally resonant. Personal stories, emotions, and experiences can provide the raw material for creating powerful lyrics and melodies that connect with listeners on a deep level.

One way that songwriters can embrace life experiences is by drawing inspiration from their own personal stories and emotions. By exploring their own experiences and feelings, songwriters can create music that is authentic and honest, and that resonates with listeners on a personal level. Writing about challenging experiences, such as heartbreak, loss, or adversity, can be a powerful way for songwriters to connect with their audience, and to provide comfort and hope through their music.

In addition to drawing inspiration from their own experiences, songwriters can also draw inspiration from the experiences of others. By observing and empathizing with the experiences of friends, family members, and even strangers, songwriters can create music that is relatable and emotionally impactful. Writing about social issues, such as inequality, discrimination, and social justice, can also be a powerful way for songwriters to use their music to effect positive change in the world.

Ultimately, embracing life experiences is a critical part of songwriting, as it allows songwriters to create music that is deeply personal and emotionally resonant. By drawing inspiration from their own experiences, as well as the experiences of others, songwriters can create music that connects with listeners on a deep level, and that has the power to uplift, inspire, and heal.

Seeking Collaboration and Feedback

Seeking collaboration and feedback is an important way for songwriters to expand their creative horizons and refine their ideas. Collaborating with other musicians and industry professionals can help songwriters to create music that is more polished, refined, and emotionally resonant. It can also help them to learn new skills, techniques, and perspectives that they can incorporate into their own work.

One way that songwriters can seek collaboration is by forming bands or songwriting partnerships. Collaborating with other musicians can help songwriters to develop new musical ideas, experiment with different styles and genres, and hone their performance skills. It can also provide valuable feedback and support as songwriters navigate the creative process.

Seeking feedback from other musicians and industry professionals is also an important way for songwriters to refine their ideas and improve their music. Receiving constructive criticism can help songwriters to identify areas where they need to improve, and to develop a clearer sense of their strengths and weaknesses as musicians. It can also provide valuable insight and perspective on the creative process, and help songwriters to develop a more nuanced and sophisticated approach to songwriting.

There are many different ways that songwriters can seek collaboration and feedback, including attending open mics, joining music communities online, and attending industry events and conferences. These opportunities can provide valuable networking opportunities, as well as exposure to new ideas and perspectives that can inform songwriting.

Overall, seeking collaboration and feedback is an important part of the songwriting process, as it can help songwriters to refine their ideas, expand their creative horizons, and create music that truly stands out. By working with other musicians and industry professionals, and by seeking feedback from a variety of sources, songwriters can improve their craft, develop a more nuanced and sophisticated approach to songwriting, and create music that connects with listeners on a deep and emotional level.

Conclusion

In conclusion, finding inspiration is a critical aspect of songwriting. By exploring different art forms, songwriters can discover new ideas and perspectives that can inform their work. Embracing life experiences can also provide a rich source of inspiration, as personal stories and emotions can be powerful tools for creating music that resonates with listeners. Seeking collaboration and feedback can help songwriters to expand their creative horizons and refine their ideas, providing valuable insight and perspective from other musicians and industry professionals. Overall, by actively seeking out inspiration and being open to new ideas and experiences, songwriters can create music that is fresh, compelling, and emotionally resonant.

Chapter 3: Crafting Meaningful Lyrics

Introduction

Crafting meaningful lyrics is a critical part of the songwriting process, as it allows songwriters to communicate their ideas, emotions, and experiences to their audience. Writing lyrics that are emotionally resonant, imaginative, and clear can help to create a powerful connection between the songwriter and the listener. To achieve this, songwriters can employ various techniques to craft lyrics that are both engaging and impactful. Tapping into emotions is one such technique, allowing songwriters to write lyrics that evoke a strong emotional response from their audience. Using imagery and metaphors can also be an effective way to make lyrics more engaging, by creating vivid mental images and comparisons that add depth and meaning. Crafting a clear message is equally important, ensuring that the listener understands the intended meaning of the lyrics and can relate to them on a personal level.

Tapping into Emotions

Tapping into emotions refers to the process of intentionally accessing and leveraging one's own emotions or the emotions of others to achieve a specific outcome or goal.

Emotions are powerful drivers of behavior, and when we understand and utilize them effectively, we can create more positive and impactful experiences.

In personal relationships, tapping into emotions can help build deeper connections and foster greater empathy and understanding. When we empathize with someone else's emotions, we can respond with greater sensitivity and create a more supportive environment. Similarly, in professional settings, tapping into emotions can be a valuable tool for leaders and managers looking to motivate their teams and drive greater engagement and productivity.

To effectively tap into emotions, it's important to first recognize and understand your own emotions. This means being willing to acknowledge and accept your feelings, even if they are uncomfortable or difficult. By doing so, you can gain greater self-awareness and develop better emotional regulation skills, which can help you navigate challenging situations more effectively.

Once you have a better understanding of your own emotions, you can begin to tap into the emotions of others. This involves actively listening to others and observing their nonverbal cues to gain insight into their emotional state. From there, you can respond in a way that acknowledges and validates their emotions, which can help to build trust and foster deeper connections.

Overall, tapping into emotions is a valuable skill that can help us build stronger relationships, enhance our communication skills, and achieve our goals more effectively. By learning to recognize and utilize emotions, we can create more positive and meaningful experiences for ourselves and those around us.

Using Imagery and Metaphors

Using imagery and metaphors involves using vivid and descriptive language to paint a mental picture for the listener or reader. This technique is used to engage the audience's imagination and make the message more memorable and impactful.

Imagery is the use of sensory language to create mental pictures for the audience. For example, instead of saying "the sun was shining," an image could be created with the phrase "the golden sunbeams danced across the shimmering waves." The use of descriptive language engages the audience's senses and makes the message more engaging and memorable.

Metaphors are figures of speech that make comparisons between two things that are not alike. For example, "he is a shining star" is a metaphor that compares a person to a star. The use of metaphors can help to simplify complex ideas and create a more relatable message for the audience.

Using imagery and metaphors can be especially effective in communication because it allows the audience to connect emotionally with the message. When we use vivid and descriptive language, we engage the listener's imagination, making the message more memorable and impactful.

This technique is commonly used in advertising and marketing to create a brand image that resonates with the target audience. For example, a car company might use the metaphor "precision engineering" to describe the attention to detail in their vehicles, creating a mental image of a well-crafted and high-quality product.

In literature, the use of imagery and metaphors is an essential tool for creating rich and complex stories. It allows writers to create a sensory experience for the reader, drawing them into the story and making it more compelling.

Overall, using imagery and metaphors is a powerful tool for enhancing communication, engaging the audience's imagination, and making messages more memorable and impactful. It is an essential skill for writers, speakers, and anyone who wants to create a message that resonates with others.

Crafting a Clear Message

Crafting a clear message is essential for effective communication. A clear message is one that is easy to understand, concise, and to the point. When we communicate with a clear message, we increase the chances that our audience will understand and remember what we are trying to say.

To craft a clear message, it's important to start by understanding the audience. This means considering their level of knowledge and familiarity with the topic, as well as their interests and concerns. By tailoring the message to the audience, we can make it more relevant and engaging.

Next, it's important to identify the key message or takeaway. This is the main point that we want the audience to understand and remember. It should be concise and straightforward, ideally no more than one or two sentences.

Once we have identified the key message, we can start to build the supporting details. These should be relevant and meaningful to the audience, and should help to reinforce the main point. It's important to avoid tangents or unnecessary information that can distract from the message.

The use of clear and concise language is also essential for crafting a clear message. It's important to avoid jargon or technical language that the audience may not be familiar with. Instead, use simple and straightforward language that is easy to understand.

Visual aids can also be a powerful tool for crafting a clear message. Graphs, charts, and images can help to illustrate complex ideas and make the message more engaging and memorable.

Overall, crafting a clear message is essential for effective communication. By tailoring the message to the audience, identifying the key takeaway, using clear and concise language, and utilizing visual aids, we can create a message that is easy to understand, engaging, and memorable.

Conclusion

In conclusion, crafting meaningful lyrics is an essential aspect of the songwriting process, allowing songwriters to convey their message and emotions to their audience. Tapping into emotions can help to create lyrics that resonate deeply with listeners, while using imagery and metaphors can add depth and nuance to the lyrics. Crafting a clear message is also important, ensuring that the lyrics are understandable and relatable to the listener. By employing these techniques, songwriters can create lyrics that are engaging, imaginative, and emotionally resonant, helping them to connect with their audience on a deeper level. Ultimately, crafting meaningful lyrics is a key ingredient in creating music that is memorable, impactful, and timeless

Chapter 4: Developing Your Songwriting Skills

Introduction

Developing Your Songwriting Skills involves honing your abilities to write lyrics, melodies, and structure songs in a way that connects with listeners. To become a successful songwriter, one needs to be able to draw inspiration from various sources, including personal experiences, emotions, and observations. This includes understanding the craft of lyric writing, which involves selecting the right words, creating vivid imagery, and developing memorable hooks. Additionally, mastering melody writing and song structure are also essential skills to create a song that flows seamlessly and resonates with the audience. In the following subtopics, we will explore each of these aspects in more detail and provide tips and techniques to develop your songwriting skills.

Finding Inspiration for Songwriting

Finding inspiration for songwriting can be one of the most challenging aspects of the creative process. As a songwriter, you need to be able to draw on a wide range of experiences, emotions, and observations to create a compelling and meaningful song. Here are some tips and techniques to help you find inspiration for your songwriting:

Personal experiences: Drawing from your own life experiences can be a powerful source of inspiration for songwriting. Think about the significant events, people, and emotions that have impacted your life, and how you can express them through your music.

Observations: Observing the world around you can also provide a wealth of inspiration for your songwriting. Pay attention to the people, places, and events that catch your eye and try to capture their essence in your songs.

Collaborations: Collaborating with other musicians or songwriters can be an excellent way to find inspiration and bring new ideas to your music. Working with other creatives can help you explore new musical styles and perspectives, and can also provide support and encouragement.

Music theory and techniques: Learning new music theory and techniques can help you break out of creative ruts and find new sources of inspiration. Experimenting with different chord progressions, rhythms, and melodies can help you create new and exciting sounds in your music.

Emotions: Emotions can be a powerful source of inspiration for songwriting. Think about the emotions that you or others have experienced and how you can express them through your music. Try to capture the essence of the emotion through the melody, lyrics, and instrumentation.

In summary, finding inspiration for songwriting requires a willingness to explore different sources of creativity and to take risks in your music. By drawing from personal experiences, observations, collaborations, music theory, and emotions, you can create compelling and meaningful songs that resonate with your audience.

Developing Lyric Writing Techniques

Lyric writing is an art form that requires practice, patience, and creativity. Whether you are an aspiring songwriter or an experienced musician, developing your lyric writing techniques is crucial to creating meaningful and memorable songs. Here are some tips to help you improve your lyric writing skills:

Start with a concept or theme: Before you begin writing lyrics, it's important to have a clear idea of what you want to express. Whether it's a personal experience, a social issue, or a universal emotion, having a central concept or theme will give your lyrics direction and focus.

Use vivid imagery: One of the most powerful tools in lyric writing is the use of imagery. By painting a picture with words, you can create a vivid and emotional connection with your audience. Use descriptive language and sensory details to help your listeners visualize your message.

Experiment with rhyme and meter: While not all songs need to rhyme or have a strict meter, experimenting with these elements can add a musical quality to your lyrics. Play with different rhyme schemes and patterns, and try writing in different time signatures to see what works best for your song.

Keep it simple: While it's important to be creative and expressive, don't let your lyrics become overly complicated or convoluted. Keep your language clear and concise, and avoid using overly abstract or obscure references that may be lost on your audience.

Edit, edit, edit: Like any form of writing, editing is crucial to refining your lyrics. Take the time to review your work, and be willing to make changes and cuts to improve the clarity and impact of your message.

By incorporating these techniques into your lyric writing process, you can develop a unique and compelling voice as a songwriter, and create songs that resonate with your audience on a deep and emotional level. Remember, the key to developing your lyric writing skills is practice and persistence, so keep writing, experimenting, and refining your craft.

Mastering Melody Writing and Song Structure

Mastering melody writing and song structure are essential skills for any songwriter looking to create music that resonates with their audience. Here are some tips to help you improve your melody writing and song structure techniques:

Start with a strong melody: A memorable melody is the backbone of any great song. Experiment with different chord progressions, scales, and intervals to create a melody that is both catchy and emotionally resonant.

Use repetition to your advantage: Repetition can be a powerful tool in melody writing and song structure. Repeating a phrase or melody can create a sense of familiarity and make your song more memorable. However, be careful not to overuse repetition, as it can also become monotonous and boring.

Play with dynamics: Dynamics refer to the variations in volume and intensity throughout a song. Playing with dynamics can add depth and emotion to your music. Experiment with building to a climax or using sudden drops in volume to create tension and release.

Think about song structure: The structure of your song can greatly impact how it is received by your audience. The most common song structures are verse-chorus-verse-chorus-bridge-chorus, or A-B-A-B-C-B. Experiment with different structures to find what works best for your song.

Collaborate with others: Working with other musicians and songwriters can bring fresh perspectives and ideas to your songwriting process. Collaborating can also help you learn from others and improve your skills.

By incorporating these tips into your melody writing and song structure techniques, you can create music that is both emotionally resonant and memorable. Remember, mastering these skills takes time and practice, so keep writing and experimenting to find your unique voice as a songwriter.

Conclusion

In conclusion, developing your songwriting skills is an ongoing process that requires practice, dedication, and creativity. By finding inspiration from various sources, developing your lyric writing techniques, and mastering melody writing and song structure, you can create powerful and impactful songs that connect with your audience. Remember, songwriting is a personal art form that requires expressing your unique voice and experiences. By developing these skills, you can tap into your creativity and bring your songs to life in a way that resonates with your listeners. With hard work and persistence, you can develop your songwriting skills and make your mark in the world of music.

Chapter 5: Writing for Different Genres

Introduction

Understanding the nuances of different genres is crucial for any songwriter looking to create music that resonates with their intended audience. Each genre has its own unique conventions and expectations, from the structure of the song to the instrumentation and lyrical themes. Adapting your writing style to fit these expectations can help your music appeal to fans of that genre, while also allowing you to experiment with new sounds and techniques. However, pushing creative boundaries within a genre can also help you stand out and create a unique sound that sets you apart from other artists. In this article, we'll explore these three subtopics in more detail, and provide tips for writing for different genres.

Understanding genre conventions

Genre conventions refer to the common characteristics and expectations associated with a particular type of media or art form, such as film, literature, or music. These conventions help audiences to recognize and understand the genre they are engaging with, and provide a framework for creators to work within. Understanding genre conventions is important because it allows us to appreciate a work of art or media within its intended context, and to evaluate it on its own terms.

Genres can be broadly defined, such as science fiction or romance, or more specific, such as a coming-of-age story or a buddy cop film. Each genre has its own set of conventions that are recognized by audiences, such as certain plot structures, themes, character types, and visual or musical elements. For example, a romantic comedy typically features a couple who initially dislike each other but eventually fall in love, and often includes humorous misunderstandings and a happy ending. A science fiction story may explore futuristic technology, alternate universes, or the implications of scientific advancements on society.

While genre conventions can be helpful in establishing expectations and creating a sense of familiarity for audiences, they can also be limiting for creators who may feel constrained by them. However, subverting or playing with genre conventions can also be a powerful tool for creating innovative and engaging works. For example, the horror film "Get Out" blends elements of horror, comedy, and social commentary in unexpected ways, creating a unique and memorable viewing experience.

In order to fully appreciate and evaluate a work of art or media, it is important to understand the conventions of its genre and how the creator has either adhered to or subverted them. By understanding genre conventions, we can better appreciate the nuances and complexities of a work, and engage with it on a deeper level.

Adapting writing style for different genres

Adapting writing style for different genres is an important skill for writers who want to effectively communicate their message and connect with their audience. Each genre has its own unique conventions, such as structure, tone, and language, which can impact how the writing is perceived and received by readers.

For example, academic writing typically follows a formal structure with clear and concise language, while creative writing allows for more experimentation with language and structure to convey emotions and ideas. A news article will have a factual and objective tone, while a memoir can be more personal and reflective.

To adapt one's writing style for a particular genre, a writer must first become familiar with the conventions of that genre. This can be achieved through reading and analyzing works in the genre, as well as researching the audience and purpose of the writing. For example, if writing for a young adult audience, the language and tone should be appropriate and engaging for that age group.

It is also important to consider the purpose of the writing. A persuasive essay will have a different tone and language than a descriptive essay. Understanding the goals and expectations of the writing can help a writer adapt their style accordingly.

Another important aspect of adapting writing style for different genres is understanding the role of the author's voice. While each genre has its own conventions, it is still important for the writer's unique voice to shine through. This can be achieved through word choice, sentence structure, and tone. A writer's voice should be adapted to fit the genre while still maintaining their own unique style.

In conclusion, adapting writing style for different genres requires a writer to be aware of the conventions of that genre and to understand the audience and purpose of the writing. It is also important to maintain the writer's unique voice while adapting to the requirements of the genre. By mastering the skill of adapting writing style, a writer can effectively communicate their message and connect with their readers across a range of genres.

Pushing creative boundaries within a genre

Pushing creative boundaries within a genre refers to the act of innovating and exploring new ideas, techniques, and themes within a particular genre. It involves breaking away from the traditional conventions of the genre and taking risks to create something new and original. Pushing creative boundaries within a genre can result in groundbreaking works that redefine the genre and inspire future artists.

One way to push creative boundaries within a genre is to experiment with the structure and form of the work. For example, a filmmaker may choose to use unconventional camera angles or editing techniques to create a new visual style, while a writer may experiment with non-linear narrative structures. This can add a fresh and unique perspective to a genre, creating a new experience for the audience.

Another way to push creative boundaries within a genre is to introduce new themes and subject matter. This can involve exploring controversial topics or tackling social issues in a new and thought-provoking way. By challenging the norms of the genre, artists can create work that is both entertaining and intellectually stimulating.

Furthermore, pushing creative boundaries within a genre requires a willingness to take risks and embrace failure. Not every experiment will be successful, but it is through these failures that artists can learn and grow. By taking creative risks, artists can develop new skills, refine their craft, and create work that is truly innovative.

In conclusion, pushing creative boundaries within a genre is a vital component of artistic expression. It involves experimenting with new techniques, exploring new themes, and taking risks to create something original and groundbreaking. By pushing the limits of the genre, artists can create work that challenges and inspires their audiences, while also contributing to the evolution of the genre itself.

Conclusion

In conclusion, writing for different genres requires a careful balance between understanding the conventions of the genre, adapting your writing style to fit those conventions, and pushing creative boundaries to create a unique and memorable sound. By doing so, you can create music that resonates with fans of that genre, while also standing out and capturing the attention of new listeners. Whether you're writing pop, rock, country, hip hop, or any other genre, taking the time to understand its nuances and expectations can help you become a more versatile and successful songwriter. With practice and persistence, you can continue to grow and develop your skills, and create music that touches the hearts and minds of your audience.

Chapter 6: Building Your Song Structure

Introduction

Introduction to Song Structure: The structure of a song is the framework that holds the music, lyrics, and melody together. Understanding song structure is crucial for songwriters and musicians, as it helps them create an organized and cohesive piece of music. In this subtopic, we'll explore the basics of song structure, including the different sections of a song and their functions.

Popular Song Structures: Many successful songs follow specific structures that have been proven to be effective in engaging listeners and conveying a message. In this subtopic, we'll take a closer look at some of the most popular song structures used in various genres, including the verse-chorus structure, the AABA structure, and the ABABCB structure.

Tips for Building an Effective Song Structure: Crafting a strong song structure can make a big difference in how a song is perceived by listeners. In this subtopic, we'll discuss some tips and techniques for building an effective song structure, such as creating a strong hook, using contrast and variation, and balancing repetition with new material. These strategies can help songwriters create songs that are memorable, catchy, and engaging.

Introduction to Song Structure

The structure of a song is the foundation that holds together the lyrics, melody, and music. Understanding song structure is crucial for songwriters and musicians, as it helps them create a cohesive and organized piece of music that engages listeners and conveys a message effectively.

At its most basic level, song structure refers to the arrangement of different sections of a song, such as the verse, chorus, and bridge. Each section of a song serves a specific purpose and contributes to the overall structure and feel of the piece.

The verse is typically the part of the song where the story or message is introduced. It often features the same melody and chords but with different lyrics for each verse. The chorus is usually the most memorable and catchiest part of a song, where the main message or theme is repeated. It typically features a different melody and chords than the verse to create contrast and make it stand out. The bridge, which is often used to connect two sections of a song, can be a moment of release or tension that breaks up the monotony of the verse-chorus structure.

Different genres of music often have their own preferred song structures, such as the 12-bar blues structure in blues music or the ABABCB structure commonly found in pop music. Understanding these structures and how they work can help songwriters and musicians make informed decisions when crafting their own music.

In addition to the basic sections of a song, song structure also includes elements such as repetition, variation, and contrast. Repetition helps to reinforce the main message or theme of the song, while variation and contrast add interest and keep the listener engaged.

In conclusion, an understanding of song structure is essential for songwriters and musicians who want to create effective and engaging music. By understanding the different sections of a song and how they work together, songwriters can craft songs that are cohesive, memorable, and emotionally resonant.

Popular Song Structures

There are several popular song structures that have been used across various genres and eras of music. These structures have proven to be effective in engaging listeners and conveying a message, and many successful songs have followed these structures.

One of the most popular song structures is the verse-chorus structure, which is commonly used in pop, rock, and country music. In this structure, the verse presents the story or message, while the chorus provides a memorable and catchy hook that ties the song together. The verses and choruses are typically repeated throughout the song, with slight variations to keep the listener engaged.

Another popular song structure is the AABA structure, which is commonly used in jazz and show tunes. In this structure, the A section presents the main melody and theme, while the B section provides contrast and variation. The A section is then repeated, followed by a bridge section that leads back into the A section.

The ABABCB structure is another popular song structure used in many genres of music. In this structure, the song alternates between two different sections, typically the verse and chorus, with a bridge section providing contrast and variation. The final section, the C section, often features a key change or different melody to provide a sense of resolution and closure.

In addition to these popular song structures, there are many other structures used in various genres of music. For example, the 12-bar blues structure is commonly used in blues music, while the call-and-response structure is used in gospel and soul music.

Understanding these popular song structures and how they work can be helpful for songwriters and musicians looking to create effective and engaging music. While there is no one "correct" song structure, these structures can provide a useful starting point for crafting a song that connects with listeners and conveys a message effectively.

Tips for Building an Effective Song Structure

Building an effective song structure is crucial for crafting a memorable and engaging piece of music. Here are some tips for building an effective song structure:

Start with a hook: The hook is the most memorable and catchy part of the song, so it's important to start with a strong hook that will draw listeners in and keep them engaged.

Vary the sections: While repetition is important in creating a cohesive song structure, it's also important to vary the sections to keep the listener engaged. This can include changing up the melody or chord progression, or adding in a new section like a bridge or breakdown.

Use contrast: Contrast is another important element in building an effective song structure. This can include using dynamics to create tension and release, or contrasting different sections of the song to keep the listener engaged.

Build towards a climax: Building towards a climax is a powerful way to create a sense of tension and release in a song. This can involve gradually increasing the intensity of the music and vocals, or introducing new elements like a key change or breakdown to create a moment of release.

Consider the lyrics: The lyrics of a song can also play a key role in the structure of the song. It's important to consider how the lyrics fit into the overall structure and how they can be used to reinforce the message or theme of the song.

Experiment with different structures: While there are many popular song structures to choose from, it's also important to experiment with different structures to find what works best for the song. This can include trying out different sections, varying the order of the sections, or creating a unique structure that suits the style and message of the song.

By following these tips, songwriters and musicians can build effective song structures that engage listeners and convey a message effectively. Whether it's through the use of repetition, variation, contrast, or experimentation, building an effective song structure is key to creating music that resonates with audiences.

Conclusion

In conclusion, understanding song structure is an essential skill for songwriters and musicians who want to create engaging and effective music. By following established structures or experimenting with new ones, songwriters can craft songs that are unique, memorable, and emotionally resonant. Whether it's the verse-chorus structure or the AABA structure, each song structure has its own strengths and weaknesses, and learning to use them effectively can help songwriters express themselves more powerfully through their music. By applying the tips and techniques discussed in this subtopic, songwriters can take their songwriting to the next level and create music that resonates with their audiences.

Chapter 7: Writing Great Melodies

Introduction

Writing great melodies is a fundamental skill for any musician or songwriter. A memorable melody can capture the attention of listeners and convey emotions and stories that words alone cannot. To write great melodies, it is important to have a solid understanding of melodic structure. This includes concepts such as phrasing, motifs, and intervals, which form the building blocks of a melody. Developing melodic ideas is the next step in the process, where creativity and inspiration play a crucial role. Finally, enhancing melodies with harmony and rhythm can take them to the next level and make them truly unforgettable. In this article, we will explore each of these subtopics in more detail and provide tips and techniques for writing great melodies.

Understanding Melodic Structure

Understanding melodic structure is essential for anyone looking to write great melodies. At its core, a melody is a sequence of musical notes that are arranged in a particular way to create a cohesive and memorable musical phrase. Melodic structure refers to the underlying organization of these notes, including elements such as phrasing, motifs, and intervals.

Phrasing is one of the most important aspects of melodic structure. It refers to the way in which a melody is divided into smaller sections or phrases, with each phrase having its own distinct beginning, middle, and end. Phrasing is what gives a melody its sense of direction and momentum, and can be used to create tension and release throughout the course of a song.

Motifs are another key component of melodic structure. A motif is a short musical idea or phrase that is repeated throughout a melody, often with slight variations or alterations. Motifs can help to unify a melody and give it a sense of coherence, as well as providing a hook or point of interest for the listener.

Intervals are the distances between the notes in a melody. Different intervals have different emotional connotations, and can be used to create different moods or feelings in a song. For example, a melody that uses mostly minor intervals might have a melancholy or introspective feel, while a melody that uses mostly major intervals might feel more upbeat and optimistic.

Understanding these elements of melodic structure is just the first step in writing great melodies. By experimenting with different phrasing, motifs, and intervals, you can create melodies that are unique, memorable, and emotionally impactful. With practice and dedication, anyone can learn to write great melodies that stand the test of time.

Developing Melodic Ideas

Developing melodic ideas is a crucial part of the songwriting process. It involves taking a basic melodic idea and expanding upon it to create a more complex and interesting melody. This process can involve experimentation with different notes, rhythms, and phrasing, as well as incorporating elements such as harmony and counterpoint.

One common approach to developing melodic ideas is to use variations. This involves taking a basic melodic idea and repeating it with slight variations or alterations. For example, you might repeat the first few notes of a melody but change the rhythm or the ending of the phrase. These variations can help to keep the melody interesting and engaging, while still maintaining a sense of coherence and unity.

Another approach to developing melodic ideas is to use chord progressions. By experimenting with different chord progressions, you can create melodies that move in interesting and unexpected ways, while still remaining harmonically grounded. For example, you might start with a basic chord progression and then add in additional chords or variations to create a more complex and interesting melody.

Counterpoint is another technique that can be used to develop melodic ideas. This involves combining multiple melodic lines that move independently of each other, creating a more complex and intricate texture. By experimenting with different counterpoint techniques, you can create melodies that are rich and layered, with multiple lines weaving in and out of each other.

Ultimately, the key to developing melodic ideas is to be open to experimentation and willing to take risks. By trying out different ideas and approaches, you can create melodies that are unique and engaging, and that truly capture the emotions and stories that you want to convey in your music. With practice and dedication, anyone can learn to develop melodic ideas and create truly memorable and impactful songs.

Enhancing Melodies with Harmony and Rhythm

Enhancing melodies with harmony and rhythm is a critical component of the songwriting process. While a strong melody can capture the listener's attention, adding harmony and rhythm can take it to the next level and create a more complete and dynamic musical experience.

Harmony is the combination of multiple notes played simultaneously, creating chords that support and complement the melody. By adding chords to a melody, you can create a more harmonically rich and interesting musical texture, and add depth and complexity to the song. Choosing the right chords to accompany the melody is crucial, as the chords can dramatically affect the emotional impact of the melody.

Rhythm is the timing and placement of musical notes within a melody. By experimenting with different rhythms, you can create melodies that are more complex and interesting, and that better support the lyrics and emotions of the song. Rhythm can also be used to create tension and release, as well as to create a sense of groove or flow within the song.

One technique for enhancing melodies with harmony and rhythm is to use counterpoint. This involves creating multiple melodic lines that move independently of each other, creating a rich and layered texture. By combining different melodic lines that move in different rhythms and with different harmonies, you can create a more intricate and interesting melody.

Another technique is to use chord progressions that move in unexpected and interesting ways. This can help to create a sense of tension and release within the song, and keep the listener engaged and interested.

Ultimately, enhancing melodies with harmony and rhythm requires a keen ear for musical texture and a willingness to experiment and take risks. By combining different elements of music and exploring different techniques and approaches, you can create melodies that are truly unforgettable and emotionally impactful. With practice and dedication, anyone can learn to enhance their melodies with harmony and rhythm and create truly memorable and engaging songs.

Conclusion

In conclusion, writing great melodies is both an art and a science. It requires a deep understanding of melodic structure, a willingness to experiment and take risks, and a keen ear for harmony and rhythm. By mastering these three subtopics - understanding melodic structure, developing melodic ideas, and enhancing melodies with harmony and rhythm - you can create melodies that are unique, memorable, and emotionally impactful. Whether you are a seasoned musician or just starting out, incorporating these principles into your songwriting process can help you unlock your full creative potential and create music that resonates with your listeners. With practice and dedication, anyone can write great melodies that stand the test of time.

Chapter 8: Arranging and Recording Your Song

Introduction

Arranging and recording a song is the process of taking a musical idea and bringing it to life in a finished recording. This involves choosing the right instruments, arranging the music for maximum impact, and recording and mixing the final product. Each of these steps requires careful consideration and attention to detail, as even small changes can have a significant impact on the overall sound and feel of the song. By understanding the key concepts and techniques involved in arranging and recording a song, you can create music that is polished, professional, and truly memorable. In this article, we will explore three key subtopics related to arranging and recording your song: choosing the right instruments, arranging for maximum impact, and recording techniques and tips.

Choosing the Right Instruments

Choosing the right instruments is a critical aspect of arranging and recording a song. Each instrument has a unique sound and timbre that can dramatically affect the overall feel and emotion of the music. When selecting instruments for a song, it's important to consider the genre and style of the music, as well as the mood and emotion you're trying to convey.

One key consideration when choosing instruments is the role they will play in the song. For example, a guitar might be used for the main melody or rhythm, while a bass guitar or keyboard might be used for the harmonic foundation. Percussion instruments like drums and shakers can be used to create a sense of rhythm and groove, while wind or brass instruments can be used to add texture and depth.

Another consideration is the range and tonality of the instruments. When selecting instruments, it's important to choose ones that complement each other and create a balanced sound. For example, if you have a high-pitched instrument like a flute or violin, you might pair it with a lower-pitched instrument like a cello or bass guitar to create a full and rich sound.

In addition to traditional instruments, there are also a variety of electronic and digital instruments that can be used in music production. These include synthesizers, samplers, and drum machines, which can add unique textures and sounds to the music.

Ultimately, choosing the right instruments is about finding the ones that best complement the song and help to achieve the desired emotional impact. By experimenting with different instruments and combinations, and listening closely to how they interact with each other, you can create a sound that is uniquely your own and truly memorable. Whether you're a seasoned musician or just starting out, choosing the right instruments is an essential part of creating music that truly connects with your audience.

Arranging for Maximum Impact

Arranging for maximum impact is about taking the individual musical elements and arranging them in a way that creates a cohesive and impactful sound. This involves considering factors such as the dynamics, instrumentation, and structure of the song, as well as the overall emotional impact that you're trying to achieve.

One key consideration when arranging a song is the dynamics. This involves creating contrast between different parts of the song to keep the listener engaged and interested. For example, you might start with a softer, more stripped-down section and gradually build to a climax with a fuller, more intense sound. This can be achieved by adding layers of instrumentation, increasing the volume or intensity of the music, or changing the rhythm or tempo.

Another consideration is the instrumentation. Choosing the right instruments and using them effectively can greatly impact the overall sound and feel of the music. For example, you might use a combination of strings and brass to create a rich, full sound, or add percussion to create a sense of rhythm and movement. It's important to consider how each instrument will interact with the others and contribute to the overall sound.

The structure of the song is also an important consideration when arranging for maximum impact. This involves deciding on the order and placement of different sections, such as verses, choruses, and bridges. By creating a clear and cohesive structure, you can guide the listener through the song and create a sense of progression and momentum.

In addition to these technical considerations, arranging for maximum impact also involves tapping into the emotional and creative aspects of music. This might involve experimenting with different melodies, chord progressions, and rhythms to create a unique and memorable sound. It's important to be open to new ideas and willing to take risks in order to create something truly impactful and memorable.

Ultimately, arranging for maximum impact requires a combination of technical skill, creativity, and intuition. By carefully considering factors such as dynamics, instrumentation, and structure, and being open to experimentation and new ideas, you can create music that truly connects with your audience and leaves a lasting impression.

Recording Techniques and Tips

Recording techniques and tips are essential for achieving high-quality recordings that capture the full range and depth of a song. Whether you're recording in a professional studio or at home, there are a variety of techniques and tips that can help you get the best possible sound.

One important consideration is the equipment you use. This includes the microphone, preamp, and recording software. It's important to choose high-quality equipment that is suited to the style of music you're recording. For example, if you're recording vocals, you might choose a microphone that is specifically designed for vocal recording and has a warm, rich sound.

Another important consideration is the acoustics of the recording space. Ideally, you want a space that has minimal background noise, good natural acoustics, and is free from echoes or other distortions. If you're recording at home, you can improve the acoustics of your space by adding acoustic treatment, such as foam panels or diffusers, to absorb unwanted sound reflections.

Mic placement is also an important consideration when recording. The placement of the microphone can greatly impact the sound of the recording, so it's important to experiment with different positions and angles to find the sweet spot. For example, when recording a guitar, you might place the microphone close to the guitar's sound hole for a more resonant sound, or closer to the neck for a brighter sound.

In addition to these technical considerations, there are also a variety of tips and tricks that can help you get the most out of your recordings. This might include techniques like double tracking, where you record multiple takes of the same part and layer them together for a fuller sound, or using effects like reverb or delay to add depth and texture to the sound.

Ultimately, recording techniques and tips are about finding the best ways to capture and enhance the unique qualities of a song. By being attentive to equipment, acoustics, mic placement, and other technical considerations, and experimenting with creative techniques and effects, you can achieve recordings that are professional-quality and truly memorable.

Conclusion

In conclusion, arranging and recording a song requires a combination of technical skill, creativity, and attention to detail. By carefully choosing the right instruments, arranging the music for maximum impact, and using the right recording techniques and tips, you can create music that truly stands out and connects with your audience. Whether you're a seasoned musician or just starting out, understanding these key concepts and techniques can help you to create music that is polished, professional, and emotionally impactful. With practice and dedication, anyone can learn to arrange and record their music in a way that truly captures their unique voice and artistic vision.

Chapter 9: Copyright and Legal Issues

Introduction

Copyright and legal issues are an important consideration for anyone creating and sharing music. Understanding the ins and outs of copyright law can help you protect your intellectual property and ensure that your work is properly attributed and compensated. Whether you're an independent artist or signed to a major label, it's important to be aware of the legal and financial implications of your music. This includes knowing how to protect your work from infringement, understanding the legal rights of other artists, and knowing what to do in the event of a legal dispute. In this section, we'll explore three key subtopics related to copyright and legal issues in music: Understanding Copyright Law, Protecting Your Intellectual Property, and Dealing with Copyright Infringement.

Understanding Copyright Law

Copyright law is the legal framework that governs the use and distribution of creative works, including music. In the context of music, copyright law protects the exclusive rights of the creator or copyright holder to use, reproduce, and distribute their work. This includes the right to control the use of their music in public performances, recordings, and other commercial uses.

As a musician or producer, it's important to have a basic understanding of copyright law so that you can protect your own work and respect the legal rights of others. This includes knowing what types of works are eligible for copyright protection (such as original songs, lyrics, and recordings), how to obtain copyright protection for your own work, and what types of uses of copyrighted music are allowed under the law.

One important concept in copyright law is the principle of fair use. Fair use allows for the limited use of copyrighted material without the permission of the copyright holder, such as for educational purposes, criticism, or news reporting. However, the exact scope of fair use is complex and can vary depending on the specific context of the use.

It's also important to understand the legal remedies available in the event of copyright infringement. This might include filing a lawsuit against the infringing party, seeking an injunction to prevent further use of the copyrighted material, or seeking damages for lost revenue.

As a musician or producer, there are a variety of steps you can take to protect your own work and respect the legal rights of others. This might include registering your own music for copyright protection, seeking permission before using copyrighted material in your own work, and being proactive about monitoring and enforcing your rights as a copyright holder.

Ultimately, understanding copyright law is an essential part of building a successful career in the music industry. By being attentive to legal requirements and being proactive about protecting your own work, you can ensure that your music is properly recognized and compensated while also respecting the rights and interests of other artists and creators.

Protecting Your Intellectual Property

Protecting your intellectual property is an important part of being a musician or producer. Intellectual property refers to the creative work that you produce, such as songs, lyrics, recordings, and arrangements. It's important to take steps to protect your intellectual property so that you can ensure that your work is properly recognized and monetized.

One key way to protect your intellectual property is to register your music for copyright protection. Copyright registration gives you legal proof of ownership over your music and the exclusive right to use, reproduce, and distribute your work. This can be important in the event of copyright infringement, as it provides a legal basis for pursuing legal action against the infringing party.

Another way to protect your intellectual property is to be vigilant about monitoring and enforcing your rights as a copyright holder. This might include regularly checking for instances of unauthorized use of your music, such as unlicensed sampling or public performances without permission. If you do discover instances of infringement, it's important to take action quickly to protect your rights and prevent further unauthorized use of your work.

In addition to copyright protection, there are other legal mechanisms available to protect your intellectual property, such as trademarks and patents. Trademarks can be used to protect your brand identity and prevent others from using your name, logo, or other identifying features without permission. Patents can be used to protect inventions or new technologies that you develop as part of your music production process.

Overall, protecting your intellectual property is an important part of building a successful career in the music industry. By being proactive about registering your music for copyright protection, monitoring and enforcing your rights as a copyright holder, and using other legal mechanisms to protect your brand and inventions, you can ensure that your work is properly recognized and monetized.

Dealing with Copyright Infringement

Dealing with copyright infringement can be a complex and challenging process for musicians and producers. Copyright infringement occurs when someone uses your creative work without permission or compensation, and it can take many forms, including unauthorized sampling, distribution, or public performance of your music.

If you suspect that your work has been infringed upon, there are several steps that you can take to address the situation. The first step is to gather evidence of the infringement, such as copies of the infringing work, witness statements, or any correspondence between you and the infringing party.

Once you have evidence of the infringement, you can send a cease and desist letter to the infringing party, informing them that their use of your work is unauthorized and demanding that they stop using it immediately. If the infringing party fails to comply with your demands, you may need to pursue legal action to protect your rights and seek compensation for any damages you have suffered as a result of the infringement.

Legal action can take many forms, depending on the circumstances of the infringement and the laws in your jurisdiction. You may need to file a lawsuit against the infringing party, seek a court order to stop the infringement, or work with a lawyer to negotiate a settlement or licensing agreement that compensates you for the use of your work.

It's important to note that dealing with copyright infringement can be a time-consuming and expensive process, and it's not always easy to prove that your work has been infringed upon. However, taking steps to protect your intellectual property and pursue legal action when necessary can help you to protect your creative work and ensure that you are properly compensated for your contributions to the music industry.

Overall, if you suspect that your work has been infringed upon, it's important to act quickly and gather evidence of the infringement. From there, you can work with a lawyer or other legal professional to take the appropriate steps to protect your rights and seek compensation for any damages you have suffered as a result of the infringement.

Conclusion

In conclusion, copyright and legal issues are an essential part of the music industry. By understanding copyright law, protecting your intellectual property, and knowing how to deal with infringement, you can ensure that your music is properly recognized and compensated. As a musician or producer, it's important to stay up-to-date with changes in copyright law and understand the legal rights and responsibilities that come with creating and sharing music. By being proactive about these issues, you can avoid legal disputes, protect your work from infringement, and ensure that your music is properly attributed and monetized. Ultimately, taking these steps can help you build a successful career in the music industry while also upholding the rights and interests of other artists and creators.

Chapter 10: Getting Your Music Heard

Introduction

As a musician, getting your music heard by a wider audience can be a challenging task. In order to succeed in the music industry, it's not enough to simply create great music - you also need to have a solid marketing strategy, a strong online presence, and a network of collaborators and industry contacts. In this section, we will explore three key areas that can help you to get your music heard: creating a marketing strategy, building an online presence, and networking and collaboration. By developing these skills and putting them into practice, you can increase your visibility and reach as a musician and connect with new fans and collaborators in the music industry.

Creating a Marketing Strategy

Creating a marketing strategy is essential for any musician who wants to get their music heard and build a fanbase. A well-planned and executed marketing strategy can help you to reach a wider audience, increase your visibility, and create buzz around your music. Here are some key steps to creating a marketing strategy:

Identify your target audience: It's important to understand who your music appeals to and what demographics you are targeting. This will help you to tailor your marketing efforts to reach the right people.

Define your brand: Your brand is your unique identity as a musician. It includes your image, message, and overall style. Developing a strong brand can help you to stand out in a crowded field and create a cohesive image that resonates with your audience.

Set goals: Identify specific goals that you want to achieve through your marketing efforts. These may include increasing social media followers, getting more streams or downloads of your music, or booking more gigs.

Develop a content strategy: Creating and sharing content is a key part of any marketing strategy. This can include social media posts, videos, blog articles, and more. Make sure your content aligns with your brand and target audience.

Choose marketing channels: There are many different channels you can use to promote your music, such as social media, email marketing, paid advertising, and more. Choose the channels that are most effective for reaching your target audience and achieving your goals.

Measure your results: Finally, it's important to track the success of your marketing efforts so you can refine and improve your strategy over time. Use tools like analytics and data tracking to monitor your progress and make data-driven decisions about your marketing strategy.

By following these steps and creating a solid marketing strategy, you can increase your visibility as a musician and reach a wider audience of fans and industry professionals.

Building an Online Presence

In today's digital age, building an online presence is crucial for musicians looking to get their music heard and connect with fans. Here are some key steps to building an effective online presence:

Create a website: A website serves as your online home base and is a great way to showcase your music, promote upcoming shows, and sell merchandise. Make sure your website is easy to navigate, visually appealing, and mobile-friendly.

Use social media: Social media platforms like Facebook, Instagram, and Twitter are great tools for building a following and connecting with fans. Use these platforms to share updates about your music, post behind-the-scenes photos and videos, and engage with your audience.

Utilize streaming platforms: Streaming platforms like Spotify, Apple Music, and YouTube are essential for getting your music heard. Make sure your music is available on these platforms and use them to promote your music to new listeners.

Build an email list: Email marketing is a powerful tool for connecting with fans and promoting your music. Encourage fans to sign up for your email list on your website or social media channels and use email campaigns to promote new releases, upcoming shows, and merchandise.

Collaborate with influencers: Partnering with influencers and other musicians in your genre can help to expand your reach and connect with new fans. Reach out to bloggers, podcasters, and other influencers in your niche and look for opportunities to collaborate on content or promotions.

By building an effective online presence, you can reach a wider audience, connect with fans, and build a successful music career. Remember to be consistent, authentic, and engaged with your audience to build a loyal following and create lasting connections with fans.

Networking and Collaboration

Networking and collaboration are essential for musicians looking to get their music heard and build their careers. Here are some key strategies for networking and collaborating effectively:

Attend industry events: Attending industry events like music conferences, festivals, and industry mixers is a great way to meet other musicians, industry professionals, and potential collaborators. Be sure to bring business cards and a positive attitude.

Join a music community: Joining a music community like a local musicians' association or online forum can help you connect with other musicians in your area or genre. These communities can provide valuable opportunities for collaboration and support.

Collaborate with other musicians: Collaboration with other musicians can help you expand your sound, reach new audiences, and build relationships with other artists. Look for opportunities to collaborate on songs, shows, or other projects.

Work with a producer or engineer: Working with a professional producer or engineer can help you take your music to the next level and open up new opportunities for exposure. Look for someone with experience in your genre and a track record of success.

Build relationships with industry professionals: Building relationships with industry professionals like agents, managers, and publicists can help you navigate the music industry and open up new opportunities. Attend industry events, network with industry professionals on social media, and seek out opportunities to work with them on projects.

By networking and collaborating effectively, you can build valuable relationships, expand your reach, and take your music career to the next level. Remember to be professional, courteous, and genuine in your interactions with others, and always look for opportunities to learn and grow as an artist.

Conclusion

In conclusion, getting your music heard in today's digital age requires a multifaceted approach. By creating a marketing strategy, building an online presence, and networking and collaborating with other musicians and industry professionals, you can increase your visibility, reach new audiences, and make important connections in the music industry. While it can be challenging to stand out in a crowded and competitive field, with persistence, creativity, and a willingness to adapt to changing trends and technologies, you can build a successful music career and share your talents with the world. Remember to stay focused on your goals, stay true to your artistic vision, and always keep learning and growing as a musician.

Conclusion

Congratulations! You've now completed the journey through "Songwriting Made Easy: A Beginner's Guide to Writing Great Lyrics in Under a Day." By working through the chapters in this book, you've learned the fundamentals of songwriting, from finding inspiration and developing your ideas to crafting great lyrics and using figurative language to make your songs more compelling.

You now have the tools you need to write great songs quickly and easily, and to take your music to the next level. Remember to always keep your passion for music at the forefront of your mind, and never stop learning and growing as a songwriter.

In addition to the skills you've acquired, you've also learned the importance of collaboration, editing, and marketing in the music industry. These skills will be crucial in helping you achieve success and build a career as a songwriter.

So, take what you've learned and apply it to your own music. Don't be afraid to experiment, try new things, and push yourself to be the best songwriter you can be. With practice, dedication, and perseverance, you can create music that moves and inspires others, and that will leave a lasting impact on the world.

Printed in Great Britain
by Amazon